President Citizen

illustrated by
Toni Goffe

Child's Play (International) Ltd

Swindon   Bologna   New York

© M. Twinn 1992   ISBN 0–85953–787–0 (hard cover)   Printed in Singapore
ISBN 0–85953–788–9 (soft cover)
Library of Congress Catalogue Number 92–259

Presidents are born.

Presidents are babies.

Presidents are toddlers.

Presidents grow up.

Presidents go to school.

Presidents take exams.

Presidents play games.

Presidents have jobs.

Presidents may get married.

Anyone can become President. Men or women.
Black. White. Any race. All religions. Healthy or sick.
Any skills or abilities. Sane or mad. You or me.
Our nation is a great mosaic of people, proud of our origins,
respecting each other, united as Americans.

You want to be President? Are you sure?
Only 1 American in 20,000,000 can ever be President.

To become President, you have to be 35. *EASY, I CAN WAIT.*
You have to be born a citizen. *THANKS, MOM AND DAD.*
You have to be elected. *MMM...*

How are people going to know about you?
You had better start right away.
It costs money to become President.

It will help
if you belong to one of the major parties:
if you are a Republican or a Democrat;

if you are already a successful politician:
a Senator or a Representative;

or if you have held public office:
as a Governor or a Judge.

It will be easier, if your ancestors came from Europe,
if you are white and male and rich,
and if powerful people are your friends.

If not, you may have to wait
a hundred years or so for your chance.
Or TRY harder.

A woman has never been nominated . . . YET!
Never a black candidate . . . YET! Never a Muslim . . . YET!

But times change.
We have come a long way fast.

It is only 500 years,
since Europeans began to colonize North America.
We only became an independent nation 200 years ago.
It is only 130 years,
since the nation was united after a civil war.

There may be a fairer system.

We could draw lots. We could take exams.

We could each take our turn
to be President for . . . TEN SECONDS.
We could let the Congress rule.

The more debate the better.
But the more people in power at the top,
the harder it is to reach a final decision.

A nation of 255 million people needs
strong leadership.

Our system may not be perfect, but it works.

Today, our country is a true democracy.
Its citizens enjoy equal rights.
The people elect the President.
The President is responsible to the people.

The President respects the Declaration of Independence.
The President respects the Constitution.
The President respects the Bill of Rights.

You don't become President for the money.

If you want wealth, there are easier ways . . .

. . . as a captain of industry, as a banker,
as the head of a crime syndicate.

You don't become President to be popular.

If you want to be loved,
be a film star, be a champion, be a dog.

But if you want POWER . . .

The President of the USA
is always in the spotlight,
the most powerful figure on the world stage.

Don't envy the President.
Being President is dangerous.
Presidents are the target of criminals, fanatics,
maniacs, well-meaning opponents, even friends.

Presidents never have a moment to themselves.

If they have even the smallest fault,
people make fun of them, or criticize them.
Especially, the press.

Nobody out-ranks the President.

Presidents cannot be experts in everything.
But they do have the best advisers in the world:
scientists, soldiers, philosophers.

Sometimes, advice can drive the President crazy.

In the end, when the President has listened,
the President alone has to decide.

Being President can be lonely.

Sometimes, Presidents make decisions,
which none of us would like to face.

Events force them to act
and bring out qualities
they did not know they possessed.

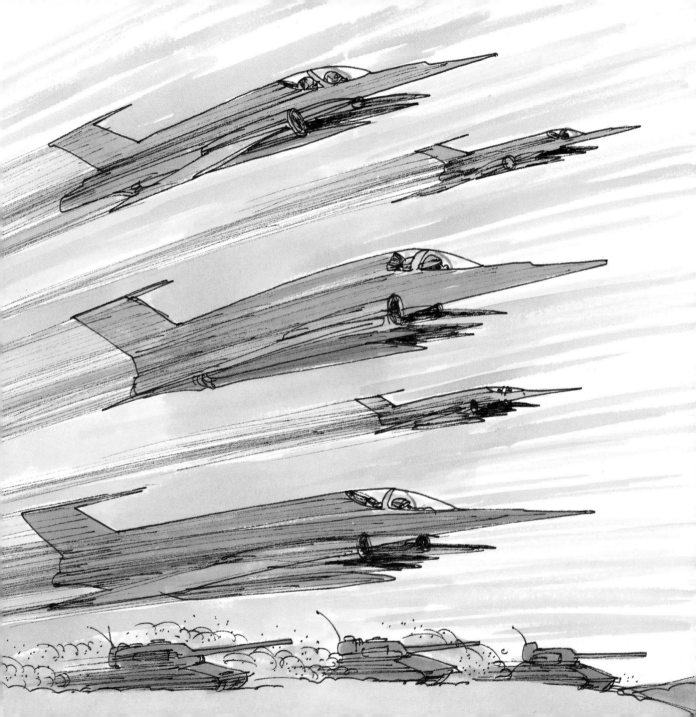

Presidents are not all Superpersons.
But they all have outstanding qualities.

Being President allows them to use them.

The best way Presidents can show their power
is to make decisions for the good of the people.

Presidents are sometimes dedicated to a cause,
to make our country a better place to live,
or to create a fairer society and a safer world.

By their example,
good Presidents bring out the best in us, too.

People make Presidents.

Presidents cannot become Presidents,
if we don't elect them.

Presidents need our vote to be nominated.
Presidents need our vote on the ballot.
Presidents need our vote to be elected.

Citizens have the right to vote, when they are 18.

As soon as we are old enough, we must use it.

We must judge carefully.
We must not be swayed
by promises
or carried away
by the excitement.

The President represents everybody.

In our system, we may not become President,
but we have the same rights.
We are citizens not subjects.

Each of us can help to ensure that our country is free,
and that children are educated,
industrious, caring and responsible.

If we are honest, we would admit
that the President does the job
as well as we could. Well, perhaps better . . .

We can't expect the President to do it all.
We have to help. We must discuss the issues
with our family and our friends, and ask ourselves,
WHAT WOULD I DO IF I WERE PRESIDENT?

We must let the President know what we think.
Through our representative in Congress.
Through the press. On the street.
In front of the White House.
Peacefully.

We don't have to wait
until we can vote.
We can be good Citizens now.

Being a good Citizen
is the first step
to becoming President.

And it is just as important!